weblinks

You don't need a computer to use this book. But, for readers who do have access to the Internet, the book provides links to recommended websites which offer additional information and resources on the subject.

You will find weblinks boxes like this on some pages of the book.

weblinks

For more information about child labour, go to www.waylinks.co.uk/ series/why/humanrights

waylinks.co.uk

To help you find the recommended websites easily and quickly, weblinks are provided on our own website, **waylinks.co.uk.** These take you straight to the relevant websites and save you typing in the Internet address yourself.

Internet safety

↗ Never give out personal details, which include: your name, address, school, telephone number, email address, password and mobile number.

↗ Do not respond to messages which make you feel uncomfortable – tell an adult.

↗ Do not arrange to meet in person someone you have met on the Internet.

↗ Never send your picture or anything else to an online friend without a parent's or teacher's permission.

↗ If you see anything that worries you, tell an adult.

A note to adults
Internet use by children should be supervised. We recommend that you install filtering software which blocks unsuitable material.

Website content

The weblinks for this book are checked and updated regularly. However, because of the nature of the Internet, the content of a website may change at any time, or a website may close down without notice. While the Publishers regret any inconvenience this may cause readers, they cannot be responsible for the content of any website other than their own.

HODDER
Wayland

Why
do people abuse
Human Rights?

Ali Brownlie

HODDER
Wayland

an imprint of Hodder Children's Books

© 2004 White-Thomson Publishing Ltd

Produced for Hodder Wayland by
White-Thomson Publishing Ltd
2/3 St Andrew's Place
Lewes
BN7 1UP

Other titles in this series:
Why are people racist?
Why are people refugees?
Why are people terrorists?
Why are people vegetarian?
Why do families break up?
Why do people bully?
Why do people commit crime?
Why do people drink alcohol?
Why do people fight wars?
Why do people gamble?
Why do people harm animals?
Why do people join gangs?
Why do people live on the streets?
Why do people smoke?
Why do people take drugs?

Editor: Philip de Ste. Croix
Cover design: Hodder Children's Books
Inside design: Malcolm Walker
Consultant: Margot Brown, Centre For Global
        Education, York St John College
Picture research: Shelley Noronha –
        Glass Onion Pictures
Indexer: Amanda O'Neill

Published in Great Britain in 2004 by Hodder
Wayland, an imprint of Hodder Children's Books

British Library Cataloguing in Publication Data
Brownlie, Ali
    Why do people abuse human rights?
    1. Human rights - Juvenile literature
    2. Civil rights - Juvenile literature
    I. Title
    323

ISBN 0 7502 4330 9

Printed by C&C Offset Printing Co. Ltd., China

Hodder Children's Books
A division of Hodder Headline Limited
338 Euston Road, London NW1 3BH

Picture acknowledgements
The publisher would like to thank the following
for their kind permission to use their pictures:
Corbis (cover), Exile Images 5 (Howard Davies), 8
(J. Etchart), 16 (Howard Davies), 25 (Howard
Davies), 29 (Howard Davies), 38 (Howard Davies),
39 (Howard Davies), 40 (Howard Davies), 45 (C.
Smith); Hodder Wayland Picture Library 4 (Gordon
Clements), 17 (Howard Davies), 18 (Angela
Hampton), 43, Mary Evans Picture Library 34;
Popperfoto/Reuters (contents) (top) (Kim Kyung-
hoon), (contents) (bottom), 6 (Ulli Michel), 11
(Danilo Krstanovic), 12 (A. Weerawong), 13 (Dan
Chung), 14, 19 (Jim Bourg), 21, 23 (Brad Bower),
24 (David Gray), 26 (Guy Wathen), 27 (Kim Kyung-
hoon), 28, 30 (Vasily Fedosenko), 32 (Jim
Hollander), 33 (US DoD), 36 (Erik de Castro), 37
(Sayed Salahuddin), 42 (Ian Waldie), 44 (Nick
Sharp); Rex Features (imprint page) (Denis
Cameron), 7 (Don Cravens, Timepix), 9 (Sipa), 10
(Sipa), 15 (Timepix), 20 (Denis Cameron), 35, 41;
Topham/ImageWorks 22, 31;

Cover picture: Workers, including a young girl,
carry bundles of wood off a boat on the Tonle Sap
River in Cambodia.

Contents

1. Understanding human rights   4

2. The right to life   10

3. Why are children's rights abused?   16

4. Why are workers' rights abused?   22

5. Why are human rights abused   28
   in times of conflict?

6. Less than human?   34

7. Upholding human rights   40

Glossary   46
Further information   47
Index   48

1. Understanding human rights

weblinks

For more information about human rights worldwide, go to www.waylinks.co.uk/ series/why/humanrights

All people have human rights simply because they are human beings. It makes no difference who they are, where they live or what they do. Human rights are like a set of rules that apply to everyone. Frequently, however, the rules are broken and human rights are violated and abused. Sometimes this is done by individuals or groups of people but often also by governments.

There is no single reason why people treat other human beings badly. On some occasions people do it on purpose because they are greedy and want to gain power or money. Some people actually like causing unhappiness to others – feelings of fear, violence and cruelty are part of all human beings in varying degrees.

◀ *Maasai people collecting water from a well. The right to clean water is denied to many people in the world through poverty and as a result of conflict.*

Sometimes people infringe on others' human rights through ignorance – they do not understand what the consequences of their actions will be. Sometimes human rights are violated when other people's rights are given a priority instead.

People often talk about the rights they think they have. They say they have a 'right' to smoke or to own a gun. These are not really 'rights' but things that people may be allowed to do by national laws. In these cases they have a legal right, but this is not the same as a universal human right. In other countries, in fact, such activities may be against the law. It is important to understand the difference between those things that all human beings need, which should be rights, and what some people would like to have or to do.

Many men and women have fought and struggled for their own rights and the rights of others, sometimes at great cost to themselves. In this book we will look at some situations where human rights have been abused.

> 'We hold these truths to be self-evident; that all men are created equal, that they are endowed by their creator with certain unalienable rights, that among these are life, liberty and the pursuit of happiness.'
> *US Declaration of Independence*

◀ *Aung San Suu Kyi addressing a rally outside her home in Rangoon, Myanmar (Burma). She has led the peaceful resistance to the military regime in Myanmar, denouncing it as a regime which has abused human rights.*

How did human rights come about?

weblinks
For more information about the rights of the child, go to www.waylinks.co.uk/series/why/humanrights

Human rights are not something new. Thousands of years ago in the ancient civilizations of Babylon, China and India people talked about human rights. Human rights have always been central to the teachings of the world's major religions.

Before the Second World War (1939–1945) it was generally felt that human rights were a matter for nations to sort out for themselves. What human rights' declarations there were did not include all members of society. For example, women and minority groups were often omitted. However the atrocities and violations of human rights that took place during the Second World War changed worldwide opinion and made them a universal concern.

▲ Nelson Mandela on his release after 27 years in prison. He stood up against the racist apartheid government of South Africa and was charged with sabotage. He became South Africa's first black president and won the Nobel Peace prize in 1993.

The people who founded the United Nations in 1945 dreamed of peace and justice through international co-operation. With this in mind the UN adopted the Universal Declaration of Human Rights (UDHR) on 10 December 1948. It is now recognized as the most important human rights document and nearly every country in the world has signed it.

case study · case study · case study · case study · case study

In Montgomery, Alabama, USA during the 1960s African-Americans and white Americans did not have equal rights. One way in which African-Americans were discriminated against was by being forced to sit in the back of public buses as a sign of respect to white people. One hot day Rosa Parks, an African-American woman, sat at the front of the bus. The driver told her to move but she refused and so the driver called for the police. Word spread about what she had done and black people stopped using the buses. The bus companies lost a lot of money because passengers had stopped using their service and eventually the rule was changed. This action was one of the springboards for the creation of the civil rights movement in the United States.

▶ *Rosa Parks (right) after the US Supreme Court ruling which said that passengers on buses should not be segregated.*

Most nations have also ratified other human rights conventions – in particular the Convention on the Rights of the Child. Unfortunately these declarations have not so far brought about an end to abuses of human rights. Since 1948 millions of people have been killed and jailed because of their origins, ideas or beliefs and for their struggles for justice and freedom. Every day of the year every single one of the 30 articles in the UDHR is being violated somewhere in the world.

7

Why abuse human rights?

It may be difficult for us to understand why anyone would abuse human rights. Some people deliberately abuse human rights because they are greedy and want power over others, or because by abusing others they can make gains for themselves. Some people abuse an individual or a group's rights because they don't believe the person or group deserves to have basic rights. An abuser may believe he or she deserves to have power over someone who is older, younger, weaker or just plain different from him or herself. Many people have an unfounded fear or dislike of those who are different from themselves.

There are also occasions where people feel forced to abuse someone else's human rights. This may be because they are trying to protect themselves and their family. Sometimes a human right is abused because the abuser believes that what they are doing is morally right, and in the interests of the greater good. For example a police officer may violate an individual's right to privacy in an attempt to catch a criminal.

▲ A protest in Chile against General Pinochet, a man who has been accused of many human rights abuses. The sign reads 'No to the devil'.

Sometimes people try to excuse human rights violations by saying that they are for the common good. In 2002 the Israeli army entered Palestinian villages and towns, bulldozed houses, and shot and arrested young men. The Israelis justified this action by arguing that it was to prevent further suicide bomb attacks in Israeli towns. This puts the rights of one group of people above those of another. Some people would argue that no abuse of human rights can be justified.

▲ *An Israeli soldier stands by while a digger removes the rubble of the demolished headquarters of the Palestinian Authority in the West Bank town of Hebron.*

2.The right to life

Is it always wrong to abuse the right to life?

Article 3 of the UDHR states that we all have the right to life. Many people believe that this is the most important right anyone can have and that it is never right to take another life.

Usually the taking of a human life is a criminal offence and is considered morally wrong, but there are exceptions. It is not always against the law and killing is sometimes justified on moral grounds. War and capital punishment are examples where killing is allowed by governments. However, nowadays capital punishment is practised in only a few countries. In some cases self-defence is recognized by the law as a justifiable excuse for killing another person, although it is often hard to prove.

◀ *The aftermath of a suicide bombing on a bus in Haifa, Israel in 2002. The bomber must have believed that the taking of human life was justified if it furthered the cause that he believed in.*

▶ *A Bosnian woman cries over her son's coffin – he was a soldier killed by Serbs near Mostar in 1996.*

In the past in some small nomadic groups of people, geriatricide (killing of the old) was practised. When times were hard and food was in short supply, elderly people were left behind when the group moved on. They would be given a small supply of food but had little hope of surviving. This was not viewed as a sign of disrespect for the elderly, and they understood that it ensured the survival of the rest of the group.

How can we distinguish between murder, manslaughter, capital punishment, killing in self-defence and killing during times of war when we are trying to decide whether the right to life has been abused? Some people argue that taking someone's life is always a violation of their right to life whatever the circumstances. But is it always wrong to kill?

FACT:
As many as 15 million children die every year from preventable diseases - 2.2 million alone from the effects of diarrhoea.
Save The Children

The right to life v. the quality of life

While many people think that the right to life is something that should never be violated, others argue that the quality of life is just as important, if not more so. Think of someone who has a terminal illness and is suffering in great pain. Should they have the right to die?

A subject which arouses great controversy is euthanasia – helping people who want to die to do so. If someone has given their permission, is it still wrong to assist them to die? People with certain religious beliefs would say it is, while humanitarians may say it is the right moral thing to do. Friends and relatives of elderly people have sometimes helped them to die or have even killed them in what they would argue was an act of mercy.

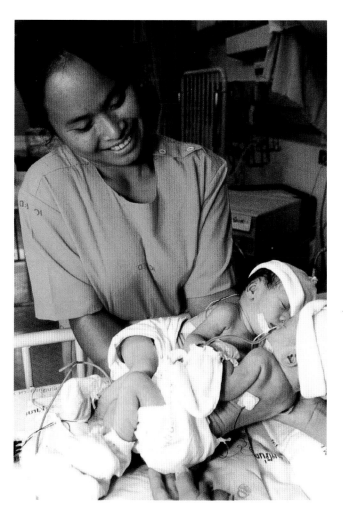

▶ *Conjoined twins at a Bangkok hospital in 1998. Sometimes one twin has to be sacrificed in order for the other one to live.*

In 2001, a British woman, Diane Pretty, went to the European Court of Human Rights to argue the case that her husband should be able to help her die without being prosecuted for doing so. She was terminally ill with motor neurone disease and had decided she did not want to live any longer and eventually die in pain. She lost her case. The ruling was that she did not have the right to die through the active intervention of another person.

▶ *Diane Pretty and her husband Brian after the verdict of the European Court of Human Rights.*

A 76-year-old in Florida shot his wife who had a terminal illness. He did it, he claimed, because he loved her and could not bear to see her suffering. He was sentenced to 25 years in prison without parole, although he was released five years later.

The issue centres on the degree to which life must be protected and the need to allow people to die with dignity and without suffering. Is euthanasia an act of kindness and compassion or an act of murder and a violation of human rights?

The state and the right to life

China is one of the countries that still uses the death penalty. This woman was convicted of murder and gasps as she hears the verdict before being taken to be executed.

During 2001 over three thousand people were killed legally by their governments through the use of the death penalty. This is practised in more than 30 countries for crimes that range from murder and treason to adultery. The countries which inflict capital punishment most are China, Iran, Saudi Arabia and the USA.

Supporters of capital punishment argue that the state should have the right to take measures that break the terms of the Universal Declaration of Human Rights. They argue that the death penalty discourages those who may murder in the future. It is also justified in terms of being 'an eye for an eye', meaning that if one life is taken, it is acceptable to take another as punishment. Some argue that murderers, who take away an individual's right to life, don't deserve to have their own rights recognized.

weblinks

For more information about the death penalty, go to www.waylinks.co.uk/ series/why/humanrights

However, those against such punishment point out that there is no evidence to show that the death penalty has reduced the murder rate. The United States, which has the death penalty, has a murder rate that is three times that of Britain which does not. People argue that governments should not have the power to decide the circumstance in which people can or should be killed. They say that to use death as a punishment is the most premeditated form of murder, and that governments are stripping people of their most fundamental right. Also, evidence has sometimes come to light later on that proves that some people sentenced to death have been innocent.

'Our present system of capital punishment violates our basic belief in justice and equality and places us among the world's worst abusers of human rights.'

Jesse Jackson Jr., US Congressman

A prisoner sits in his cell on death row in Angola State Prison, Louisiana, USA.

FACT:
In 2001, 66 prisoners were executed in the USA, bringing the total to 785 since 1976.
Amnesty International

3. Why are children's rights abused?

Children's rights – special rights?

Children, as human beings, are entitled to basic human rights, although in the best interests of the child, adults usually make decisions on their behalf. What happens to a child in her or his early years will influence how the rest of their childhood and adulthood unfolds. Children need good nutrition, education and care. According to the United Nations about 150 million children in the world under the age of five are malnourished. This is a direct result of poverty – one of the most common obstacles to the enjoyment of basic human rights.

Like other groups in society that lack power and are vulnerable, children are often denied their rights. They have little say in things that affect them. They are often expected to do things and are treated in a way that would be seen as an abuse of rights if an adult were treated in the same way. Examples range from not being listened to or taken seriously to being forced to work in terrible conditions or to fight in wars.

▲ *Children need special care. This child is being weighed as part of a programme in Kenya run by Médecins sans Frontières, an international medical aid organization.*

Children are denied some of the rights adults have because they are thought too young to be able to exercise them responsibly, and they need special protection. For instance, children are not allowed to vote, or get married under a certain age. This age varies from country to country.

Clearly, children need special protection. For this reason, in 1989, the United Nations adopted the Convention on the Rights of the Child. It recognized the important differences between adults and children. All but two of the world's 193 nation states – the USA and Somalia – have ratified and signed up to the Convention. The American government, however, believes that the Convention undermines parental rights.

'The principle of "all children, all rights" is still too far from being a reality.'

Kofi Annan, UN Secretary General

weblinks

For more information about child/youth rights, go to www.waylinks.co.uk/ series/why/humanrights

▼ *Children enjoying a game of football in Jamaica. The Convention on the Rights of the Child says that all children should have the right to play.*

Child cruelty and abuse

Children are dependent on the adults who look after them. This dependency, and their lack of physical power, make children particularly vulnerable to physical and sexual abuse and neglect. On occasions children are beaten, forced into sexual acts, or not provided with proper food, warmth, shelter, clothing, care and love.

While the vast majority of adults who look after children do a good job, there are a few who abuse the trust that children and society allow them. Shockingly it is sometimes the parents who are responsible for child abuse. Foster parents, clergy, teachers, and neighbours are also among the adults who have been convicted of abusing children at some point.

There is evidence to show that some abused children go on to be abusive parents and that some sex offenders, particularly those who target children, experienced sexual and physical abuse in their own childhood. However, other children suffer terrible childhoods but do not grow up to be abusers themselves.

▶ *A child with Down's Syndrome. Children with disabilities have particular needs; in school they may be targeted by bullies.*

In many countries where it would be illegal to hit an adult, it is permissible to smack children as a form of punishment. How and when adults can do this to children depends on the national laws.

▲ Protesters demonstrate against the sexual abuse of children by members of the clergy in Boston, USA.

Children themselves sometimes abuse the rights of other children particularly through bullying and name-calling. Bullies may sometimes be people with a low opinion of themselves. Bullying is a way to try and hide this from other people. As in adults though, some child bullies are those who believe they have special, or more, rights than their peers.

FACT:
On any one day in the USA it is estimated that over 3,000 school students will experience some form of physical punishment.

Child labour

During the nineteenth century in England some children were made to work in factories, mines and mills for up to 12 hours a day. Because they were small they were made to crawl into cramped places to do difficult and dangerous work. Many children were injured or killed. Children were cheap to employ and the factory owners made good money.

Today approximately 250 million children aged between 5-17 years old work worldwide, often in conditions no better, and sometimes worse, than those experienced by children in the nineteenth century. Their families live in poverty and they send their children out to work from a young age. They do many different jobs. For example, they may weave carpets, where their small hands are able to do delicate work, or stitch footballs. They earn just a few pennies a day. Rarely are there any regulations covering the conditions in which they work. They may toil for 16 hours a day without a break.

weblinks

For more information about child labour, go to
www.waylinks.co.uk/
series/why/humanrights

▼ *A child working in Egypt. Even very young children may be required to operate dangerous machinery in cramped unhealthy conditions.*

Young people participating in the six-month Global March arriving outside the International Labour Organization headquarters in Geneva, Switzerland. Young people from all over the world joined in the march against child labour.

Grinding poverty forces these children into work – for them it is a necessity. Although child labour is against the law in countries like India, it still goes on where factory owners are determined to use cheap child labour to increase their profits. People in the western world are not always aware of the role they are playing in supporting this practice when they buy products like footballs and trainers. Poverty lies at the core of this abuse of human rights.

'I have been stitching soccer balls as long as I can remember. My hands are constantly in pain. It feels like they are burning.'
Geeta, aged 11, India

4.Why are workers' rights abused?

Work as a right

Work is the way in which people are able to earn money to meet their basic needs and keep themselves alive. Work can also be fulfilling and contributes to a person's feelings of worth. Article 23 of the UDHR states that people should have the right to work, to do so in decent conditions, to enjoy equal pay with someone who is doing the same job, and to receive a wage that is fair for the type of work being done. The Article also states that everyone has the right to form and join a trade union. These are 'economic rights'.

▼ People on their way to work in New York City. The UDHR states that everyone has a right to work.

Larry Jones, a former employee of Coca-Cola, campaigned against the company which had been accused of discriminating against black people.

In most countries of the world it is the job of the government to ensure that there is work. If the economy begins to fail, job losses follow and unemployment rises. But sometimes people find it difficult to get work even when there are plenty of jobs around. This is when it becomes a human rights issue because it means that people are being discriminated against. This usually happens on the grounds of the race, sex, age, religion, disability or the sexual orientation of the person seeking work.

Although in many countries it is against the law to discriminate in this way, some companies find ways round it. For example, a company in the north of England did not want to hire black people, so it invented a policy of not employing people from a particular area of a city because it knew that many black people lived there. In Brazil some companies require women to produce a certificate of sterilization when applying for a job, so they will not need to have time off work in order to have a baby.

FACT:
In the UK black people are twice as likely to be unemployed as white people, even if they are better qualified to do a certain job.
International Labour Organization

Rights versus profit

The basic purpose of business in a capitalist system is to make a profit. Most companies recognize that to do this they must respect human rights; after all, it benefits their business in the long term to do so. But in some cases the bosses are so driven to increase their profits and keep their own highly paid jobs that they ignore the rights of the workers.

> FACT:
> The largest companies in the world - such as Wal-Mart, ExxonMobil, General Motors - have revenues larger than the economies of entire middle-income countries, such as Norway, Poland and Denmark.

At least 1.1 million people around the world die of work-related accidents and diseases each year. Even more are injured. Many of these deaths and injuries could have been prevented if the companies had spent more money and taken more care to ensure there were adequate health and safety provisions.

◀ A May-Day anti-globalization protestor dressed as a 'Fat Cat' outside the Australian Stock Exchange in Sydney 2001. 'Fat Cat' is the name given to a boss who takes a huge salary and bonuses from his company.

A protestor in London demonstrating her objections to an Arms Trade Fair in London supported by the British Government. The purpose of such fairs is to sell weapons and armaments to other countries.

The activities of one particular business may not violate human rights, but in seeking to make a bigger profit they may choose to buy their supplies from companies that do abuse rights. For instance, a company making chocolate may buy their ingredients from another company that uses forced child labour in the cocoa plantations of West Africa. Other businesses may produce products that are used to violate human rights. This is especially true of the arms industry, which produces landmines that remain lethal long after they have been laid. In the chemical and pharmaceutical industries, drugs may be tested on people in poorer countries where there are fewer regulations to protect their safety.

Some large tobacco companies target children and adolescents to encourage them to take up smoking even though it has been proved that cigarette smoking causes death. In developing countries free cigarettes are handed out in the streets in the hope that people will take up the habit.

Trade unions

The terrible and dangerous conditions in which many people worked in the factories and workshops of nineteenth-century Europe led to the founding of trade unions. Workers realized that there was strength in numbers and got together to negotiate with employers for improvements in pay and conditions. They also began to put pressure on governments to create laws that would protect their rights as workers.

▶ *A miner is rescued from a flooded shaft at the Quecreek Mine in Somerset, Pennsylvania in 2002. Miners face particular dangers in their jobs.*

case study · case study · case study · case study · case study

In 1888 Anne Besant wrote a newspaper article called 'White Slavery in London' about the dreadful pay and dangerous conditions suffered by young women working at the Bryant and May match factory. Three girls suspected of giving her information were sacked – and 1,500 women walked out in sympathy. The firm gave in. Many countries now have a legal minimum wage – a small formal recognition of union demands for human dignity. Nowadays, people like Anne Besant who draw public attention to abuses in the workplace are known as 'whistle-blowers'.

Article 23 of the UDHR states that 'everyone has the right to form and join a trade union…'. However forming trade unions has not always been easy. Although unions are there to defend the rights of workers, in some countries actually working for or belonging to a trade union can lead to imprisonment, torture or even death. Even when trade unions are accepted, people can still lose their jobs or be victimized for trying to set up a trade union. In Colombia the leader of a paramilitary group said that trade unionists should be killed because they interfered with the 'orderly conduct of business'.

In 1984 the British Government announced that staff at GCHQ, a spy station that listens in to communications around the globe, had to resign from their union or face dismissal. The reason given by the government was that being a member of the union might be in conflict with national security. Many refused to give up their right to belong to a union and lost their jobs. In this instance people's right to belong to a union was considered to be less important than national security.

▶ *Members of the Federation of Korean Trade Unions hold banners during a rally in Seoul on 1 May 2002. The demonstrators were demanding a shorter working week.*

27

5. Why are human rights abused in times of conflict?

The causes of war

War is the greatest threat to people's human rights. Inevitably people are killed and injured but there are many other human rights casualties too. People are traumatized, and forced to leave their homes and become refugees. People's freedom is limited and usually severe restrictions are put on the media and what they are allowed to report. All wars create poverty and human suffering. In Sudan, for example, six million people were displaced during the 1980s, the majority as a result of food shortages due to disruption to farming and trade.

> **FACT:**
> More than 120,000 children under the age of 18 are being used as soldiers in Africa.
> *Human Rights Watch, 1999*

◀ *During the border tension in Kashmir, a territory between India and Pakistan that both countries claim, Pakistani soldiers listen to a briefing from General Khan, 2002.*

The causes of war are complex and varied. They include conflict over land ownership, as in the dispute between India and Pakistan over Kashmir, or a battle of beliefs and ideologies, like the Korean War between the communist-backed North Korea and the US-backed South Korea in the early 1950s. Today Korea is still divided into North and South.

Most wars have both historical and human causes. They are the result of things that have happened in the past and of how people view the current situation. On several occasions wars have been sparked off by a single event. Old rivalries and tensions between the Hutus and Tutsis in Rwanda flared into conflict, genocide and massacres when the president, Juvenal Habyarimana, was killed in a plane crash. Hutus suspected that this was the work of Tutsi rebels. It is estimated that more than 500,000 Rwandans died and over half the surviving population was forced to move from their homes as a result.

> 'We must remember that these faithful followers [of the Fascist leaders]… were not born torturers, were not (with a few exceptions) monsters, they were ordinary men.'
>
> *Italian novelist Primo Levi, survivor of Auschwitz, 1987*

◀ *Rwandan refugees crossing the river to Tanzania in 1994, fleeing the genocide in Rwanda when Hutus and Tutsis were killing one another.*

The human rights of civilians

During the twentieth century civilians have increasingly become the victims of war and armed conflicts. As hand-to-hand fighting becomes less common and the military make use of long-distance rockets and bombing from the air, civilians are more often in the firing line.

Civilians are often forced to flee wars and conflict zones, becoming refugees and asylum seekers. They leave behind their homes and possessions, sometimes even their families, and become one of the world's most vulnerable groups. Many of their human rights are denied them, particularly their right to security (Article 3) and their right not to be exiled (Article 9).

Human rights are further infringed when a state of emergency is declared in a country. During this time the media may not be able to report what is going on, people may be subjected to a curfew, restricting their right to freedom of movement and being part of a community.

weblinks

For more information about campaigns against censorship, go to
www.waylinks.co.uk/series/why/humanrights

▶ *Afghan refugees wait for food at a camp in Koja Bahuddin in north Afghanistan in 2001. They were forced from their homes by fighting.*

FACT:
The countries that received the most refugees in 2000, relative to their total population, were Armenia, Guinea, Yugoslavia and Congo.

'You cannot explain what it is like to be forced from your home. I just wanted to cry and never stop.'

Saranda, Kosovo

The public often supports censorship in certain circumstances believing it to be in the interest of their own security. But this can be open to abuse. Organizations like Article 19, named after the relevant article in UDHR, campaign against any kind of censorship. They argue that the free reporting and investigation of issues by journalists is the cornerstone of democracy.

Journalists themselves run risks in reporting. In 1998 50 journalists were killed around the world, 22 of them in Latin America. This was usually as a result of their investigations taking them too close to people who had something to lose by being exposed.

▶ *A Palestinian helps a photographer who has been shot in the hand during clashes with Israeli troops in 2000.*

War atrocities

Soldiers and people who serve in the military are vulnerable to human rights abuses on two fronts. On the one hand they are put into dangerous positions where they may be ordered to commit atrocities, and on the other they are vulnerable to having their own rights abused.

When war is declared one of the first things that may happen is that able-bodied civilians are conscripted, or forced to join the military. Some countries accept that people have the right to refuse to fight and these people may be required to work in civilian service, such as in a hospital.

> 'As a pacifist I object to any army. I will never carry a weapon and I refuse to wear a uniform or any symbol that represents or labels me as part of the army.'
> *Yair Halper, aged 18, imprisoned in Israel for resisting the draft*

▼ *A group of Israeli conscripts – Israel is one of the countries where young people have to serve in the army.*

In the early 1960s a study was conducted at Yale University. Researchers found that volunteers of all ages and occupations would willingly follow orders to inflict pain on other people. Although the volunteers were troubled by the pain they were inflicting, they were also convinced that they were involved in a worthwhile scientific experiment. Studies like this have now been banned in US universities, but they teach us a valuable lesson about why ordinary people sometimes commit horrible human rights abuses.

weblinks

For more information about agencies that help the victims of war, go to www.waylinks.co.uk/series/why/humanrights

In time of war, soldiers who are trained to obey orders will behave in ways that they would find unthinkable in other circumstances. At My Lai in 1968, during the Vietnam War, American soldiers obeyed orders given by Lieutenant William Calley to kill hundreds of unarmed men, women and children at close range.

Soldiers themselves have their rights protected by the Geneva Convention. First written in 1864, this sets out the terms and conditions under which the wounded and prisoners of war should be properly treated in times of war.

▽ *These prisoners were detained during fighting in Afghanistan and are being held at Camp X-Ray at the US naval base in Guantanamo, Cuba. The conditions under which they are being kept appear to contravene the Geneva Convention.*

6. Less than human?

Dehumanization

weblinks

For more information about an organization that tries to protect the rights of minority groups around the world, go to www.waylinks.co.uk/series/why/humanrights

One of the worst cases of human rights' abuses the world has ever seen was the Holocaust, the organized genocide of six million Jews, and five million other people including Roma (gypsies), the mentally ill and homosexuals and communists, by the Nazis during the Second World War.

The Nazi philosophy was based in part on the ideas of Ernst Rudin. He was a psychiatrist who believed that 'inferior' people should be separated from the rest of the population to create a 'better' society. This would involve either keeping them in special places and preventing them from having children, or killing them. These chilling ideas were not that unusual in the early part of the twentieth century and were fully believed by the Nazis. In the 1920s and 1930s Germany was in the grip of an economic crisis. The Nazis used people's fears about the economy and the state of the country to turn them against Jews and other minority groups.

▶ *During the Second World War, Jews were shipped to concentration camps in conditions not even fit for animals.*

A grieving woman tends the grave of her husband, killed in the conflict in Bosnia in the 1990s.

A modern-day holocaust occurred during the war in Bosnia in the 1990s. The Serbian military commander, Ratko Mladic, ordered his troops to shell particular villages because Muslims lived there. Similarly in Rwanda in 1994 the government, which was led by people from the Hutu population, ordered the massacre of 800,000 Tutsis. Nowadays, policies and actions such as these which target particular ethnic groups are known as 'ethnic cleansing'.

This habit of thinking of people who are different as less than human has been a constant problem in human history. This 'dehumanization' is a key element in much wartime propaganda. It is the basis of racism and nationalism and makes it much easier to motivate troops to fight. It is also used to justify slavery and racial discrimination.

> 'They have killed gays and lesbians in Texas because they believe them to be less than human. I believe it is very important that people understand why murders happen and that such murder is a result of hatred… these murderers were taught to hate by society.'
>
> *Ann, a human rights campaigner, Texas*

In the name of religion?

Article 18 of the UDHR states that 'everyone has the right to freedom of thought, conscience and religion; this right includes freedom to change his religion or belief, and freedom, either alone or in community with others and in public or private, to manifest his religion or belief in teaching, practice, worship and observance.'

◀ *An anti-Taliban Afghan fighter prays hours before the end of Ramadan – the Islamic month of fasting – in Afghanistan in 2001.*

Throughout history this right has been denied many people. For a period of 350 years between the fifteenth and nineteenth centuries the Spanish Inquisition ordered the torture and murder of thousands of Spanish Jews, Muslims, Christians and homosexuals who were punished for not believing in the orthodox Catholic Doctrine.

Under the Taliban rule in Afghanistan women were required to cover themselves completely by wearing a burqa, whether they wanted to or not.

And today, in the twenty-first century, people still have their right to worship denied to them. In China, members of Falun Gong, a spiritual movement, have been imprisoned for their beliefs by the Government. In Tibet, which is governed by China, many Buddhist monasteries have been destroyed and monks have been expelled and taken to China for 're-educating'. Some have been tortured for practising their religion.

On some cases people have tried to force their own religion on others. In 1099 Christian crusaders swept into Jerusalem after a five-week siege and massacred many of the city's Muslims and Jews. They forced their own religion on the rest. More recently, in the 1990s, the Taliban regime in Afghanistan denied young girls the right to go to school and to work. On occasions, it killed men for not attending prayers. These acts were carried out in the name of religion.

A woman's lot

Women make up half the world's population yet they do two-thirds of the world's work, earn one-tenth of the world's income and own less than 1 per cent of the world's property. And all over the world women contribute hugely to the world's economy through their unpaid work in the home.

Yet in many societies women are considered to be inferior. Around the beginning of the twentieth century some psychologists believed that women were less highly evolved and less intelligent than men. This theory has been totally disproved although women still have less power and influence than men in many walks of life.

▲ *This poster in Cambodia warns of the problem of violence against women.*

case study · case study · case study · case study · case study

In April 1999 29-year-old Samia Sarwar, the mother of two young children, was shot dead in the office of her lawyer in Lahore, Pakistan. She was seeking a divorce after suffering years of violence at the hands of her husband. But, shockingly, her own family was to blame. Family members felt that by seeking a divorce she was bringing dishonour on the family, so they arranged for an assassin to kill her. She was shot in the presence of her own mother and uncle.

Women's rights are abused on a daily basis throughout the world. Quite a lot of women are victims of physical abuse committed by their partners at some time in their lives. In many countries the law fails to protect women from this kind of abuse. In the worst cases women have been killed.

Some research has gone into exploring why men abuse women. What this suggests is that it is a way for men to assert power and control over women. But another reason must be that men can often get away with domestic violence. The criminal justice system in most countries does little to protect women.

▲ *A Palestinian woman at a training centre. Training programmes help women to take control of their lives.*

FACT:
It is estimated that one in four women will experience some form of domestic violence at some point in their lives.

weblinks
For more information about the problem of violence against women in the home, go to www.waylinks.co.uk/ series/why/humanrights

7. Upholding human rights

Human rights and international law

Human rights apply to every single person in the world. But human rights are abused all over the world. In some cases the laws of a country are at odds with recognized human rights. For example, some countries have the death penalty, even though that goes against the right to life. Another example may be laws which attempt to stop people from making racist statements – these laws can be seen as going against the right to free speech. This is why international conventions and agreements are so important and so complicated.

Most countries have their own laws that protect people's human rights and they have also signed the various international conventions. But the United States has consistently resisted signing and ratifying the Convention on the Rights of the Child, claiming that their own domestic laws are adequate. It resents what it sees as interference from the international community.

Women at a literacy class in Bengal, India. Women in many countries learn to read and write as adults as the right to education was denied them when they were young.

▲ *Slobodan Milosevic on trial at the International Criminal Tribunal for the Former Yugoslavia. He was accused of crimes against humanity in Kosovo.*

The United States has been reluctant to support the setting up of the International Criminal Court. This court will punish leaders of countries which abuse human rights and will prosecute people accused of genocide, crimes against humanity and war crimes. The US thinks the court may be used to accuse its soldiers of human rights' abuses.

On an individual level it is vitally important that people learn what their rights are and become confident to challenge those who try to take them away. Education is the key to helping people stand up for their rights.

66 'We must rid this planet of the obscenity that a person stands a better chance of being tried and judged for killing one human being than for killing 100,000.'

Jose Ayala-Lasso, UN Commissioner for Human Rights, 1996

99

Conflicting human rights

Libertarians believe that everyone should be free to do as they choose, as long as they do not interfere with the freedom of others. But human rights often conflict with each other and with people's beliefs and faiths and national laws. Sometimes these conflicts prevent human rights from being upheld.

The right to freedom of expression or a fair trial may clash with the right to privacy. Celebrities often see the freedom of the press as infringing on their right to privacy. The right to cultural or religious practice may clash with the right not to be discriminated against. The rights to a healthy environment, education, health care or welfare benefits may be in competition with one another over the same limited resources.

Some people claim that Princess Diana's death was caused because her car was being chased by press photographers. She often complained that her privacy was invaded by cameramen.

There are often conflicts between individual and group human rights. In order to feed its rapidly growing population, in 1980 China introduced a 'One Child Policy'. Every birth had to be approved by family planning officials. The family received free education, housing, pension and other benefits but these were withdrawn if they had a second child.

In a similar way some countries, such as Australia and Belgium, demand compulsory voting in general elections. The purpose is to ensure democracy, but is it an infringement of someone's freedom to force them to vote?

▲ In China, families are only permitted to have one child. The government argues that this is in the best interests of the majority.

Bystander or activist?

It is easy to think that none of us will abuse someone else's human rights. Yet there is a saying that goes 'all that is needed for evil to prevail is for good people to do nothing.' In other words failing to take action against someone who is abusing rights can be as bad as deliberately abusing human rights yourself. Every person has to take responsibility for the consequences of their actions and ensure that they are not harming others. We should also seek out ways in which we can guarantee the human rights of others.

In 1995 the United Nations sent peacekeeping forces into Bosnia to protect the local population which was being threatened by Serbian forces. In the event the Dutch forces were accused of human rights abuses for not doing enough to protect the population of the town of Srebrenica. Up to 8,000 Muslim men and boys were executed by Serb soldiers while the 100-strong Dutch UN contingent did nothing to save them.

▶ *Dutch UN peacekeeping forces resting next to Bosnian refugees from Srebrenica, 1995. The Dutch troops did not prevent the killing of Muslims who were under their care.*

weblinks

For more information about ways in which young people can help to change and improve the world, go to www.waylinks.co.uk/ series/why/humanrights

Businesses can be guilty of indirectly abusing the human rights of their own military forces. In the late 1980s US and European countries sold chemical and biological weapons to Iraq. Since the Gulf War more than one in three of the US troops who served there have sought medical care for undiagnosed problems, possibly related to toxic exposures to chemicals.

Human rights cannot be guarded simply by individuals, businesses and the state not interfering with individual freedoms. The human rights of people have to be actively fought and campaigned for. The best way to do this is through education. All of us should make efforts to learn more about this important subject.

▲ *Driving while drunk endangers other people's human rights. This is a memorial to a victim of a drunk driver in California, USA. The organization 'Mothers Against Drunk Drivers' (MADD) was set up to highlight this problem.*

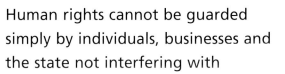

'Rights for too many remain little more than words on paper. However, I do believe that we should commit ourselves to focusing on the future, reinvigorating the common will and commitment of the international community to ensuring the enjoyment of human rights by people everywhere. We are all custodians of human rights and we must find our own way to do what is required.'

Mary Robinson, High Commissioner for Human Rights, United Nations

GLOSSARY

Abortion
The deliberate early ending of a pregnancy before a baby is born.

Adultery
Sexual relationships outside marriage.

Apartheid
Segregation of a population on the basis of their colour.

Atrocity
A cruel and inhumane deed.

Boycott
To refuse to have anything to do with someone or a group of people.

Capital punishment
The act of putting someone convicted of a crime to death.

Capitalism
An economic system that depends on the private ownership of property.

Censorship
The banning of certain information from being published or broadcast.

City state
A fortified city in Ancient Greece which was self-governing.

Civil rights
Rights that all citizens have. They include legal, economic and social rights.

Civil rights movement
The campaign to secure equal rights for Afro-Americans and black people in the United States.

Civilian
Someone who is not connected with the military forces of a country.

Conjoined twins
Twin babies that are physically joined together at birth.

Conscientious objector
Someone who refuses to serve in the armed services on ethical grounds.

Conventions
International agreements.

Curfew
An order stating the time by which people must be at home.

Democracy
Government elected by the people; from the Greek word *demos* which means 'people' and *kratos* which means 'rule'.

Discrimination
Unfair treatment of someone usually because of their race, gender, sexual orientation or disability.

Doctrine
A set of beliefs.

Down's syndrome
A congenital disorder resulting in a person having a flat face and some learning difficulties.

Ethnic cleansing
The act of mass expulsion or killing of people from ethnic or religious groups in a certain area.

Euthanasia
The act of killing someone painlessly, often because they are suffering an incurable illness. Sometimes called 'mercy killing'.

Genocide
The mass killing of a particular racial or cultural group.

Holocaust
An act of great destruction and loss of life. Commonly used to describe the extermination of eleven million Jews, Roma (gypsies), mentally ill and gay people by the Nazis during the Second World War.

Humanitarians
People devoted to promoting the well-being of other human beings.

Ideology
A system of political or philosophical beliefs.

Infringe
To break a set of rules.

Libertarians
People who believe that other people should be able to do what they want freely.

Manslaughter
The unlawful killing of another person.

Massacre
Mass murder.

Minority group
A group of people who are racially different from the larger group of which they are a part.

Negotiate
To discuss something with another party in order to reach an agreement.

Pacifist
Someone who is opposed to all forms of violence.

Paramilitary
A group of people who are not in the armed forces, but who are organized and behave like a military unit.

Parole
To release a prisoner before their sentence is complete on the promise of good behaviour. People on parole are still checked on by the authorities.

Ratification
The formal approval and granting of legal authority to a document.

Refugee
Someone who is forced to leave their home and country against their will.

Segregated
Being forced to lead a life separate from other people.

Sterilization
An operation that prevents women from getting pregnant.

Trade union
An organization set up to protect the rights of workers.

Universal
Something that applies to everyone in the world.

Violate
To go against a previous agreement.

BOOKS TO READ

For children

Historical Storybooks: Freedom Song, the Story of Nelson Mandela by Neil Tonge (Hodder Wayland, 2002)

One Day We Had to Run by Sybella Wilkes (Evans Bros in association with UNHCR and Save the Children, 1997)
The experiences of refugee children through their own eyes.

Peace Begins With You by Katherine Scholes (Little Brown and Co, 1994)
An explanation of how and why peace has a place in all of our lives. It explores the many ways in which conflicts can be resolved.

Stand Up for Your Rights (Two Can Publishing, 1998)
A compilation of stories, experiences and pictures illustrating the articles of the UDHR. Produced by young people.

The Long Walk to Freedom (Amnesty International, 2000)
A coloured wall chart of human rights' defenders around the world.

The Universal Declaration of Human Rights by Ruth Tocha and Otavio Roth (UN, 1990)
An illustrated book that adapts the original text of the Universal Declaration of Human Rights into easier language for children.

Viewpoints: A Right to Die? by Richard Walker (Franklin Watts, 1997)

What Do We Mean By Human Rights? (Franklin Watts, 2000)
Five illustrated background readers on different human rights topics including Freedom of Belief, Freedom of Speech, Freedom of Movement and Equal Rights.

World Organisations by Reg Grant (Franklin Watts, 2000)
Includes titles on the United Nations, UNICEF and Amnesty International.

For teachers

Have I The Right? (Charter 88, 1988)
Information pack on the Human Rights Act (UK) and its importance for young people.

Freedom! Human Rights Education Pack (Amnesty International and Hodder & Stoughton, 1998)
A comprehensive teaching pack including information on women's rights, torture and genocide.

ORGANIZATIONS

Amnesty International
99 Rosebery Avenue
London EC1R 4RE

Anti-Slavery International
Unit 4, Stableyard
Broomgrove Road
London SW9 9TL

British Red Cross
9 Grosvenor Crescent
London SW1X 7EJ

Charter 88
16-24 Underwood Street
London N1 7JQ

Equal Opportunities Commission
Overseas House
Quay Street
Manchester M3 3HN

Liberty
21 Tabard Street
London SE1 4LA

Minority Rights Group
379 Brixton Road
London SW9 7DE

Oxfam
274 Banbury Road
Oxford OX2 7DZ

Refugee Council
3 Bondway
London N1 9PD

Save the Children
17 Grove Lane
London SE5 8RD

Survival International
6 Charterhouse Buildings
London EC1M 7ET

UNHCR
8-14 Avenue de la Paix
1211 Geneva 10
Switzerland

WEBSITES

For websites that are relevant to this book, go to www.waylinks.co.uk/series/why/humanrights

INDEX

Numbers in **bold** refer to pictures.

Afghanistan **30**, **33**, **36**, 37, **37**
Armenia 31
arms industry 25, **25**
Article 19 31
Aung San Suu Kyi **5**
Australia 43

Bangkok **12**
Belgium 43
Besant, Anne 26
Bosnia **11**, 35, **35**, 44, **44**
Brazil 23
Britain 15, 27
Buddhism 37
bullying 19
Burma see Myanmar

Calley, Lieutenant William 33
Cambodia **38**
Camp X-Ray **33**
capital punishment 46
capitalism 24, 47
censorship 31, 46
child abuse 18, 19
child labour 20, **20**, 21, **21**, 25
children's rights 16, 17
Chile **8**
China 6, 14, **14**, 37, 43
civil rights 7, 46
Colombia 27
concentration camps **34**
Congo 31
conscription 32, **32**
Convention on the Rights of the
    Child 7, 17, **17**, 40
curfews 30, 46

death penalty 9, 11, 14, **14**, 40
Denmark 24
Diana, Princess **42**
Down's Syndrome **18**, 46
drugs testing 25

Egypt **20**
ethnic cleansing 35, 46
European Court of Human Rights
    13
euthanasia 12, 13, 46

Falun Gong 37
Federation of Korean Trade Unions
    27

GCHQ 27
General Motors 24
Geneva **21**
Geneva Convention 33, **33**
genocide 29, 34, 41, 46
Germany 34
Global March **21**
Guantanamo **33**
Guinea 31
Gulf War 45
gypsies 34

Habyarimana, Juvenal 29
Haifa **10**
Hebron **9**
Holocaust 3, 46
homosexuals 34, 37
Hutus 29, **29**, 35

India 6, 21, **28**, 29, **40**
International Criminal Tribunal for
    the Former Yugoslavia **41**
International Labour Organization
    21
Iran 14
Israel **10**, 32, **32**
Israelis 9, **9**, **31**, 32

Jamaica **17**
Jerusalem 37
Jews 34, **34**, 37
Jones, Larry **23**

Kashmir **28**, 29
Kenya **16**
Khan, General **28**
Koja Bahuddin **30**
Korean War 29
Kosovo **41**

Mandela, Nelson **6**
manslaughter 11
Médecins sans Frontières **16**
mentally ill people 34
Milosevic, Slobodan **41**
minimum wage 26
Mladic, Ratko 35
murder 11, 13, 14, **14**, 15
Muslims 35, 37, 44, **44**
Myanmar **5**
My Lai 33

Nazis 34
New York City **22**

Norway 24

Pakistan **28**, 29
Palestine 9, **9**
Palestinians **31**, **39**
Parks, Rosa 7
Pinochet, General **8**
Poland 24
poverty **4**, 16, 20, 21, 28
Pretty, Diane 13, **13**

racism 23, **23**, 40
Rangoon **5**
refugees 28, **29**, 30, **30**, 31, 46
Roma 34
Rudin, Ernst 34
Rwanda 29, **29**, 35

Saudi Arabia 14
Second World War 6, 34, **34**
segregation **7**, 46
Seoul 27
Serbs **11**, 35, 44
sexual abuse 18, **19**
smoking 25
Somalia 17
South Africa 6
Spanish Inquisition 37
Srebrenica 44, **44**
Sudan 28
suicide bombing **10**
Sydney **25**

Taliban **36**, 37, **37**
Tanzania **29**
Tibet 37
torture 27
trade unions 22, **22**, 26, 27, **27**, 46
Tutsis 29, **29**, 35

United Nations 6, 16, 17, 44, **44**
Universal Declaration of Human
    Rights (UDHR) 6, 7, 10, 14, 22, 27,
    31, 36
USA 7, 14, 15, **15**, 17, **19**, 40, 41, **45**

Vietnam War 33

war 10, 11, 16, 28, 29, 30, 32, 41
West Africa 25
women's rights 6, 38, **38**, 39, 40
workers' rights 22, 23, 24, 26, 27

Yugoslavia 31